also by Alicia Young

Hell on Heels
*Fried Chicken, Schmussy, and other
Songs from a Baptist Hymnal*

The Death of Disco

poems by
Alicia Young

Poetic Justice Books & Arts
Port Saint Lucie, Florida

©2018 Alicia Young

book design and layout: SpiNDec, Port Saint Lucie, FL
cover design: Billy Burgos, Los Angeles, CA

All rights reserved.

No part of this book may be used or reproduced in any manner whatsoever without written permission except in the case of brief quotations embodied in critical articles and reviews. Members of educational institutions and organizations wishing to photocopy any of the work for classroom use, or authors, artists and publishers who would like to obtain permission for any material in the work, should contact the publisher.

Printed in the United States of America.

Published by Poetic Justice Books
Port Saint Lucie, Florida
www.poeticjusticebooks.com

ISBN: 978-1-950433-094

The Death of Disco was originally published as a limited edition chapbook by Poetic Justice Books in 2018.

*To James,
who came later,
and decided to stay forever.
Thanks for that.*

The Death of Disco
Alicia Young

contents

indentations	3
detail oriented	4
america the dutiful	5
across the ohio	6
Frankencock	7
See Rock City	8
fainting goat	9
big trains	10
cinemascope	11
city confidential	12
nom noms	13
we never had paris	14
number two	15
contentment & vine	16
place settings	17
last call	18
uprooted	19
in lieu of flowers	20
the t-shirt	21

indentations

i never met a typewriter
i didn't want to bang

detail oriented and self motivated supreme being seeks management position with room for upward mobility

god has failed
to live up to his résumé
since the germinal moments
of the industrial age
yet somehow
he keeps getting
a pay raise

america the dutiful

when we are unwilling
to sacrifice for the greater good
the greater good
becomes the sacrifice

across the ohio

when the oxycodone and meth crops fail in kentucky
the country folk flock
across the ohio river into cincinnati
to go to the open air opioid market
people once came to the queen city from the south
to get factory jobs that no longer exist
they were called briar hoppers
we don't have a name for these new immigrants
other than marginalized, homeless, inmate, and DOA's
but they're good at making change
a five dollar bill on the streets of this town
will turn into a baggy of heroin
faster than it will turn to singles

Frankencock

Hugh Hefner is dead
at 91
but his dick
is being kept alive
in the Playboy Mansion
so future generations
of starry-eyed young women
will not be deprived of the misery
of riding his withered antique
liver spotted genitalia
into a career of middling infamy
and sexual exploitation

See Rock City

how far man has come
from the moment
we were a trillionth the size
of a mote of dust
sunbeam suspended
matter dancing out of existence on
antimatter stripper poles
super-heated
into the biggest bang ever to blow
horny comets
into hadrons of extinct dinosaurs
dead shopping malls
kamikaze day traders
perched atop
financial district temples
sky diving down to
urine caked sidewalks
radicalized soccer moms
suicide bomb drum majors
high stepping into
Russian voting booths
and sheepy suburbanites
willing to eat hot artichokes

fainting goat

every day
with him
was the last day

big trains through small tunnels

it struck me
as funny
that free condoms
handed out in
New York City
had subway maps
on the wrappers
in case you were erect
and desperately needed
to get
to Yonkers

cinemascope

he loved me
the way film
can make death
beautiful

city confidential

i'm guilty
of compartmentalizing
my life
no one will know each other
at my funeral
Robert Stack will narrate
the unsolved mysteries
there will be several unknown
oddly distraught
handsome gentlemen
friends from all over
and family
who will conduct it
like a senate hearing

nom noms

men are
comfort food

we never had paris

his oxfords stroll down
piano key sidewalks
stepping to quarter notes
noir film
thoughts smoldering
behind him in cigarette smoke
and i think
in another life
we would have fallen in love
during wartime

number two

he loved everything
in pencil

contentment & vine

when you find the corner
of contentment & vine
chaos comes as a dark-eyed lover
yellow cab splashing
through the crosswalk puddle
leaving you nothing but dripping regrets
and the keys to an apartment building
still burning

place settings

I thought that I loved you,
but it was just your talent for lying
over candlelight.

last call

the moon
looks like
someone
stood her up
tonight

uprooted

you can sit at a table
drinking wine
palms flat to the wood
without remembering
that table was ever a tree
but my heart will never forget
it bled for you
once

in lieu of flowers

the doctor asked
if i wanted a death certificate
i said yes
proof of life
that she existed
as you can't bury
lost hope
in a tiny white casket

the t-shirt

when next the situation arises
that i need to sleep at your place
and i borrow something to sleep in
don't give me sweats or your best pajamas
i want your oldest, rattiest t-shirt
the Nirvana t-shirt that you bought
in 1992 from a record store
back when there were record stores
the one your mom spilled bleach on
so you didn't take it to band camp
but it was okay because bleach
was their best album
the t-shirt that mopped up
your barf in college
the one your roommate spilled
both ranch dressing and candle wax on
at the same party
the one that's faded from being washed 7,000 times
that needed washing a few more
the t-shirt that has a constellation
of holes in it that look
like the Falkland Islands
the t-shirt your dog had puppies on
but you cleaned that shirt and kept wearing it
because you love that dog
and you loved those puppies
and it made you want to keep
that fuckin' t-shirt even more
give me that soft broken-in
raggedy t-shirt
that represents your entire life
give me that t-shirt
to sleep in

Alicia Young lives in Cincinnati with her husband, James, twin sons, Chandler and Gabriel, and her cats, John Henry and Ruby. She is an employee of the Public Library of Cincinnati and Hamilton County. She is the author of two previous books of poetry, *Hell on Heels, poems by Alicia Young* (Lady Lazarus Press, 2012), and *Fried Chicken, Schmussy, and other Songs from a Baptist Hymnal* (Leaky Boot Press, 2016).

www.ingramcontent.com/pod-product-compliance
Lightning Source LLC
Chambersburg PA
CBHW030105100526
44591CB00008B/275